MACMILLAN TYPING TASK

Displays & Tal

Paul Bailey

© Paul Bailey 1979

First edition 1979
Reprinted 1981, 1982

Published by
THE MACMILLAN PRESS LTD
London and Basingstoke
Companies and representatives
throughout the world

British Library Cataloguing in Publication Data

Bailey, Paul, b. 1937 (Dec.)
    Displays and tabulations. – (Macmillan typing
    task books).
    1. Typewriting
    I. Title
    652.3   Z49

    ISBN 0-333-26209-3

Printed in Hong Kong

TYPING TASKS - DISPLAYS AND TABULATIONS

This book of some 20 simple displays and 97 tabulations has been compiled to provide a wide range of supplementary material to complement any basic typing text and in particular *Typing for Colleges for elementary and intermediate examinations* and *Comprehensive Typing*. It provides material for use by teachers who prefer not to use a basic text but who teach from their own material. The exercises range from the very simple to the intermediate standard of the public examining bodies.

The book has been compiled so that all exercises can be used in a number of ways - blocked or centred display, alphabetical and numerical order, with leader dots, ruled - and so on. Although instructions are given for all exercises it is anticipated that teachers will give students further instructions as required - the Contents page shows the range of topics covered and can be used as an exercise in its own right. Most of the exercises are in simple manuscript in order to provide the further exercise of reading it.

Together with the other two books which complete this present series - *Typing Problems* and *Letters, Postcards and Memoranda* - this book provides a comprehensive series of exercises which lead directly to the taking of public elementary and intermediate examinations.

The author wishes to thank Margaret Hewines for editing and members of the staff of T P Riley School for providing the handwriting.

CONTENTS

Page

Simple displays 4
Menus 7
Advertisements 11
Simple display in columns 14
Headed column work 19
Numerical order 21
Chronological order 22
Headed tabulations 25
Tabulations using the brace 61
Tabulations with horizontal lines 63
Simple boxed ruled tabulations 76
Boxed ruled tabulations with headings 79
Ruled tabulations with multi-line headings ... 85

Paper: A5 (210 x 148 mm).
Display to best advantage.

REQUIRED

RECEPTIONIST/TELEPHONIST

Mature person able to type

Normal office hours

Apply:

HENRY SQUIRE & SON
Temple Way
BRISTOL
BS99 7DH

Telephone: Bristol 72740

Paper: A5 (148 x 210 mm).
Display to best advantage.

Due to further expansion we require a YOUNG LADY/MAN (aged 16-18)

Knowledge of French and German required

Typing an advantage

Good opportunity for an enthusiastic person

Written applications only

ROCKWELL TRANSLATIONS

26 Mill Lane

TRURO

TR1 3BA

Paper: A5 (148 × 210 mm).
Display to best advantage.

J. S. LANCASTER

21a High Street, Newport.
(1st Floor Queen's Buildings)

Newport 97971 and 24877

Join our satisfied clients

Save money

Leave your insurance worries to us

PAY BY INSTALMENTS

Check the rates and ask for a quote

N O W!

Paper: A5 (210 × 148 mm).
Display.

Enjoy a Greek night out at

THE ACROPOLIS

RESTAURANT

Anchor Parade
Barnstaple

Wine, dine and dance to
Bouzouki Music

For details telephone:

Barnstaple 35061

Display on a sheet of A5 (148 x 210 mm) Display on a suitable sheet of paper.
paper.

PRIMEWOOD PROPERTIES LIMITED 20   GENERAL OFFICE WORK

Leave 2 clear lines   Leave 2 clear lines

Entries are now being invited for 23   Accurate typing essential

A SALE OF ANTIQUE 17   Shorthand/Audio not required

PICTURES/FURNITURE/SILVER 25   Small switchboard

ETC   3   General filing

To be held on 13   Interesting job with excellent
                                        conditions
Wednesday 19 April at 21
                                           Leave 3 clear lines

The Saleroom 19   Telephone: Sheffield 27491
Brickhill Drive 15
Rugby 5

Leave 2 clear lines

Closing date for entries 2 April 32

Display each of the following 12 menus on suitable sheets of paper.

JANUARY

Onions à la Greque

x x x

Tenderloin of Pork with Apricot Sauce
Sauté Potatoes
Broccoli Spears au Gratin

x x x

Iced Tangerines

x x x

Coffee

FEBRUARY

Crème de Coquilles St. Jacques

* * *

Chicken Maryland, garnished with
bacon rolls and watercress
Chipped Potatoes
Tossed Green Salad

* * *

Citron Fromage with Fresh Cream

* * *

Tea or Coffee

MARCH

Minestrone Soup

Avocado Pears with Prawns

—

Veal Scaloppine
Duchesse Potatoes
French Beans

—

Zabaglione

—

Tea or Coffee

APRIL

French Turnip Soup

Chicken Liver Pâté

—

Salmon Steaks with Cream
Buttered New Potatoes
Lettuce and Cucumber Salad

Chilled Almond Soufflé

—

Coffee

MAY

Tomato Ice

—

Lobster Thermidor served with
Crisp French Bread and
Tossed Green Beans

Grapefruit in Brandy

—

Coffee and Petits Fours

JUNE

Asparagus in Mornay Sauce

—

Gammon with Apricot Stuffing
Buttered Potatoes
Creamed Spinach

Blackcurrant and Mint Pie
with Fresh Cream

—

Coffee

JULY

Stuffed Eggs Provençale

* * * *

Noisettes of Lamb
            Shrewsbury

Boiled New Potatoes
Courgettes

* * * *

Raspberry Yoghourt
            Sorbet

* * * *

Iced Tea

AUGUST

Gazpacho Andaluz

* * * *

Salade Niçoise

* * * *

Jambon à la Crème
Boiled Potatoes
Salad

* * * *

Lemon Syllabub

* * * *

Coffee

SEPTEMBER

Melon and Ham Gondolas

* * * *

Crab Puffs

* * * *

Grouse à la Grandmère
Creamed Potatoes
Cauliflower Polonaise

* * * *

Hazel Nut Gantois

* * * *

Tea or Coffee

OCTOBER

Fruit Juice

* * * *

Wild Duck with Mandarins
Roast Potatoes
Buttered Green Beans

* * * *

Apple and Nut Strudel

* * * *

Coffee with Petits Fours

NOVEMBER

Game Soup with Port Wine

Honeydew Cups

Tournedos en Croûte

Scalloped Potatoes

Turkish Fried Carrots

Fresh Figs with Yoghourt

Tea or Coffee

DECEMBER

Crème Vichyssoise

Eggs in Provençal Sauce

Pork Chops with Almonds and
Sherry

Creamed Potatoes

Brussels Sprouts with soured
cream

Apple-Rum Meringue

Tea or Coffee

Paper: A5 (148 x 210 mm). Display to best
advantage.

BARTON-ON-SEA
Recorded Music Society
PROGRAMME

Finnish Fantasy - Glazanov
Moscow Radio Symphony Orchestra - Boris Khaikin

Piano Concerto No.2. - Rachmaninoff
New York Philharmonic Orchestra - Leonard Bernstein
Soloist - Gary Graffman

The Planets - Holst
Vienna Philharmonic Orchestra and the
Vienna State Opera Chorus - Herbert von Karajan

Symphony No.3 - Nielsen
London Symphony Orchestra - Francois Huybrechts

Concert starts at 7.30 p.m.

Members admitted free

Guests are asked to make a donation

Paper: Suitable. Display.

TOWN HALL
KETTERING

12th May at 7.30 pm

ROYAL LIVERPOOL PHILHARMONIC ORCHESTRA

Conductor: Walter Susskind

Overture: Fingal's Cave – Mendelssohn
Piano Concerto in D minor – Mozart
(Soloist: Walter Susskind)

Symphony No.5   – Schubert
La Mer   – Debussy

Tickets at the usual prices.

Box office: KETTERING 82924

Paper: Suitable. Display.

FESTIVAL HALL

6 February at 1930 hours

THE HALLÉ ORCHESTRA

Conductor: James Loughran

Overture: In the south – Elgar

Harold in Italy – Berlioz
(Soloist: William Lincer)

Symphony No. 3 – Harris
The Birds   – Respighi

Tickets through the usual agents or at the Box Office

Paper: A5 (148 x 210 mm). Display.

WELLSBURY & CO
Chartered Auctioneers, Valuers and Estate Agents
20/22 Park Avenue
WORKSOP
Nottinghamshire
580 3AP
Telephone: Worksop 2520
PARK FARM
WORKSOP

To be sold by auction at the field gate
on Monday 16th May at 7pm

44,209 ACRES OF GRAZING LAND

Lot 1 - 17,861 acres
Lot 2 - 10,602 acres
Lot 3 - 15,746 acres

The grazing is for cattle only

Particulars and plan from the above

Paper: A5 (210 x 148 mm).

Afghan	Collie	Labrador
Alsatian	Dachshund	Mastiff
Beagle	Greyhound	Pointer
Borzoi	Husky	Spaniel

Paper: A5 (210 x 148 mm).

Aardvark	Bandicoot	Coypu
Acuchi	Bat	Dormouse
Agouti	Beaver	Gerbil
Alamiqui	Capuchin	Gopher
Aluata	Cat	Hare

Paper: A5 (210 x 148 mm). Arrange the names in
alphabetical order.

Austria	Switzerland	Malta
Finland	France	Holland
Iceland	Italy	Belgium
Norway	Denmark	Wales
Portugal	Spain	Scotland
Sweden	Greece	Ireland

Paper: A5 (210 x 148 mm). Arrange the names in
alphabetical order.

Nile	Tiber	Colorado	Seine
Thames	Yana	Fraser	Oise
Congo	Rakaia	Ganges	Rhine
Amazon	Darling	Sungari	Tagus
Trent	Parana	Ural	Severn
Mississippi	Negro	Indus	Oder

Paper: A5 (210 x 148 mm).

Apricot Beauty	Princess Elizabeth	Red Shine
Brilliant Star	Red Pitt	Red Emperor
Prince of Austria	Sunkist	Sweet Harmony
Orange Nassau	China Pink	Paris
Scarlet Cardinal	Ellen Willmott	Berlioz

Paper: A5 (210 x 148 mm).

Brussels Sprouts	Chili	Lettuce
Cabbage	Chicory	Leek
Cape Gooseberry	Cress	Marrow
Carrot	Cucumber	Melon
Cauliflower	Egg Plant	Onion
Celery	Kohl Rabi	Sweet Corn

Paper: A4. Type the following list of countries in alphabetical order in two columns using double-line spacing.

Hungary	Egypt	Ethiopia	Gabon
Italy	Kuwait	India	Greece
Fiji	Afghanistan	Indonesia	Japan
Guinea	France	Denmark	Chile
Belgium	Brazil	Austria	Burma
Zambia	Nigeria	Malta	Syria
Spain	Turkey	Mexico	Sweden
Kenya	United Kingdom	Sudan	Tanzania
Mali	Tunisia	Norway	Paraguay
Thailand	New Zealand	Libya	Luxembourg
Senegal	Uruguay	Canada	Cuba
Belize	Laos	Iceland	Jamaica
Honduras	Iraq	Uganda	Cambodia
Bolivia	Cyprus	Peru	Singapore
Togo	Pakistan	Australia	Tonga

Paper: Suitable.
Type the following list of elements in two columns
in alphabetical order.

Cobalt	Tin	Silicon
Wolfram	Iodine	Mercury
Uranium	Sulphur	Potassium
Chlorine	Copper	Zinc
Helium	Radium	Gold
Calcium	Fluorine	Argon
Magnesium	Vanadium	Carbon
Oxgyen	Nitrogen	Neon
Boron	Sodium	Phosphorus
Nickel	Hydrogen	Aluminium
Plutonium	Lead	Strontium
Silver	Thallium	Tungsten

```
Paper: Suitable.
Display the names of the stalls in alphabetical
order.  Justify the right-hand margin.
```

SUMMER FÊTE

STALLS

Tombola   Pots and Pans

Coconut Shy   Toffee Apples

Roll a ball   Football

Cake stall   Treasure Island Chase

Plant stall   Mops and Cans

Balloons   Pony Rides

Coin in a Bucket   Tractor Rides

Aunt Sally   Buzz Wire

Find the Egg   Goldfish

Dart the Card   Bottle stall

Crazy kitchen   Golf

Teas, Ices, Hot Dogs, Hamburgers
and Soft Drinks available
GRAND OPENING   1.30 pm

Paper: Suitable.
Display with justified left and right margins.

STRANGE AFFAIR

<u>Characters in order of appearance</u>

Jadwiga Tredar	Mabel Fox
Adokwei Tetteh	Devereux Chavasse
Julius Sajiwandani	Arthur Onyejekwe
Marion Rao	Owen Joshi
Driver	Stephen Outer
Passenger	Kamal Bulos
Guard	Tristan Benac
Ogoja Angiama	Eban Akanni
Sheila	Dorothea Pavlitski
Stanislaus Gomez	Fitzroy Kowlesser
Rabinder	Natu Kapur
Guard	Leo Wildi
Doris	Patricia Rozee
Nicholas Odantzis	Jonathan Kamm
Helen La Vie Grant	Barbara Akaot
Peter Zagni	Evans Obeng-Asamvah

Paper: A5 (210 x 148 mm).
Display in numerical order.

62	14	99
28	100	4
16	2	25
101	66	13
74	48	37
20	57	81
29	83	70

Paper: A5 (210 x 148 mm).
Display in numerical order.

3892	5827	3785	2472
3416	5429	5334	4672
2414	2186	6229	3545
2908	2910	3039	2236
5221	3793	5727	3127
2639	4933	6522	2192
4760	5213	2438	6053

Paper: Suitable. Type the sailing dates in
chronological order in 3 columns.

SAILING DATES

Southampton - Cherbourg - New York

August 5	June 29	September 21
November 28	October 31	August 28
April 26	May 16	June 17
September 9	July 11	August 16
June 5	October 3	July 23

Paper: Suitable. Type the sailing dates in
chronological order in 4 columns.

SAILING DATES

New York - Cherbourg - Southampton

November 18	September 14	September 26
July 28	November 5	August 10
September 2	June 10	
May 29	July 4	
August 21	October 16	
April 17	July 16	
June 22	May 1	

Paper: A5 (210 x 148 mm).
Display in chronological order.

YEARS

1802	1944	1492
1937	1555	1112
1812	1763	1886
1746	1891	1697
1066	1608	1783
1272	1378	1707
1485	1592	1314
1506	1947	1296

Paper: Suitable.
Arrange the following in chronological order.

Person	Year of Birth	Person	Year of Birth
John Adams	1735	William Booth	1829
Joseph Addison	1672	Elizabeth Browning	1806
Roald Amundsen	1872	Robert Bunsen	1811
Hans Andersen	1805	Robert Burns	1759
Jane Austen	1775	John Cabot	1425
Baden-Powell	1857	Anton Chekov	1860
William Baffin	1584	Samuel Colt	1814
Irving Berlin	1886	Gabriel Fahrenheit	1686
William Bligh	1754	Henrik Ibsen	1828

23

Paper: Suitable.
Arrange the programmes into the correct order
according to time.

TODAY'S PROGRAMMES

7.00 pm	The early evening film (The Time Machine)
11.30 am	Cartoon time
6.00 pm	The news
1.05 pm	The news
10.30 pm	The news
8.50 am	Time for the under five's
9.15 pm	New ideas in industry
11.45 pm	Life under the sea - exploring for oil in deep water
9.40 am	Disco time
6.20 pm	Variety show
12.15 pm	The 10 to 20 show
1.20 pm	Afternoon sport Show jumping Racing Football Results
9.45 pm	The chase - Part 5
1.30 am	Close down
11.00 pm	The late film - The Return of Time
5.00 pm	New variety Talent show
8.45 am	Holiday weather

Paper: A5 (210 × 148 mm).

KINDS OF BATS

African Crested	Californian Mastiff	Flittermouse
Bare-backed Fruit	Carnivorous	Flying Fox
Big Brown	Dog-faced	Ghost
Black Tomb	Falcon	Great Northern
Bulldog	Fish-eating	Guano
Butterfly	Flat-faced Fruit	Jackass

Paper: A5 (210 × 148 mm).

KINDS OF DOG

Boston Terrier	Dingo	Old English Sheepdog
Bull Terrier	English Setter	Pekinese
Chihuahua	Great Dane	Russian Collie
Coonhound	Irish Wolfhound	Saint Bernard
Dalmatian	Kerry Blue	Yorkshire Terrier

Paper: suitable.   Arrange the towns into alphabetical order.

SOME EUROPEAN TOWNS

Genoa	Brussels	Seville	Palma	Angers
Athens	Amsterdam	Nantes	Tours	Toledo
Barcelona	Copenhagen	Milan	Dresden	Leon
Lisbon	Hamburg	Reims	Ayr	Chartres
Bordeaux	Berlin	Dublin	Hannover	Padua
Paris	Stockholm	Vienna	Amiens	Siena
Florence	Bergen	Bologna	Cork	Turin

Paper: A5 (210 x 148 mm). Arrange the trees and shrubs into alphabetical order.

TREES AND SHRUBS

Clematis	Cornus	Prunus	Spiraea
Laburnum	Daphne	Lilac	Potentilla
Hydrangea	Rhus	Wisteria	Mulberry
Buddleia	Holly	Cedrus	Jasmine
Rosa	Rhododendron	Malus	Cytisus
Pyracantha	Willow	Skimmia	Cotoneaster

Paper: Suitable. Display the following.

Colour	Flower	Day	Time of Year
Jade Green	Rose	Saturday	Winter
Grey, violet	Crocus	Thursday	Winter
Scarlet	Lily of the Valley	Tuesday	Spring
Pink and blue	Hyacinth	Friday	Spring
Lemon	Primrose	Wednesday	Spring
Silver	Rose	Monday	Summer
Red and blue	Carnation	Sunday	Summer
Gold	Rose/Orchid	Wednesday	Summer
Blue/Burgundy	Carnation	Friday	Autumn
Crimson	Chrysanthemum	Tuesday	Autumn
Blue/Purple	Violet	Wednesday	Autumn
Turquoise blue	Iris/Orchid	Saturday	Winter

Paper: Suitable. Display the following.

UNITS OF VOLUME

Metric Units

Cubic millimetre

Microlitre

Cubic centimetre

Millilitre

Centilitre

Decilitre

Cubic decimetre

Litre

Cubic metre

British Units

Bushel

Register Ton

Cubic Yard

Pint

Quart

Gallon

Drachm

Peck

Gill

United States Units

Bushel

Shipping Ton

Cubic Yard

Pint

Quart

Gallon

Dram

Peck

Gill

Paper: A5 (210 x 148 mm).

COLOUR AND TRIM COMBINATIONS

Body Colours	Trim Colours	Coachline Colours
Strato Silver 13	Black or Tan	Grey or Orange 14
Celtic Bronze 13	Black or Tan	Gold
Saturn Red 10	Black or Red	Black or Red
Ice Blue	Black or Gold 2	Black
Mint Green	Red or Tan	Black or Gold 15
Snow White	Black or Red	Black or Red
Buttercup Yellow 19	Black or Tan	Black
Black	Black or Red	Gold

Paper: Suitable. Display.

THE ZODIAC

DATES

SIGN	DATES	BIRTHSTONE
Aquarius	January 20 - February 18	Opal / Green Jade
Pisces	February 19 - March 20	Emerald
Aries	March 21 - April 20	Ruby
Taurus	April 21 - May 20	Rose quartz
Gemini	May 21 - June 20	Topaz / yellow diamond
Cancer	June 21 - July 21	Pearl
Leo	July 22 - August 21	Diamond
Virgo	August 22 - September 21	Yellow diamond / sardonyx
Libra	September 22 - October 22	Sapphire
Scorpio	October 23 - November 21	Ruby
Sagittarius	November 22 - December 20	Amethyst
Capricorn	December 21 - January 19	Turquoise

Paper: Suitable. Type the tabulation in 3 columns in alphabetical order.

MOBILE HOMES

CHECK LIST

Door Mat 1	Kettle 1	Ashtrays 2
Butter Dish 1	Water Carrier 1	Fire Extinguisher 1
Saucers 4	Plates, Small 4	Cruet 1
Potato Peeler 1	Bucket 1	Dish Cloth 1
Teapot 1	Bread Bin 1	Milk Jug 1
Tin opener 1	Pillows 4	Bread Knife 1
Plate, meat 1	Fish slice 1	Spoons, Tea 4
Spoons, Table 4	Spoons, Dessert 4	Brace 1
Egg Cups 4	Tea Caddy 1	Frying Pan 1
Knives 4	Forks 4	Cups 4
Bread Board 1	Grill Pan 1	Tea Cloths 2
Sugar Basin 1	Floor Cloth 1	Bowl (Washing up) 1
Pudding Basins 2	Tea Strainer 1	Coffee Grinder 1
Plates, Large 4	Scouring Pad 1	Saucepans 2
Table Spoon 1	Mantles 2	Door Keys 2
Hand Brush 1	Dust Pan 1	Coffee Pot 1
Regulator 1	Gas Cylinders 2	Tumblers 4
Blankets 8	Sheets 8	Coathangers 8

HOME FREEZING GUIDE

Vegetable	Boiling time (minutes)
Asparagus	2-4
Aubergines	3-4
Beans: broad	2-4
dwarf	2-3
runner	2-3
Broccoli	3-5
Cabbage, shredded	1-2
Carrots: diced	2-4
whole	4-6

Vegetable	Boiling time (minutes)
Cauliflower, sliced	2-4
Celeric, sliced	2-4
Celery, sliced	2-4
Parsnips, diced	2-4
Peas	1-2
Spinach	1-3
Sprouts	2-5
Sweet corn (Maize)	6-7
Turnips, diced	2-3

Fruits should not be blanched — treat with white sugar before freezing.

Paper: Suitable.

A GUIDE TO GROWING FLOWERS

Flower	Sow	Depth mm	Germination Period
Alyssum	March - April	6	7 - 10 days
Aquilegia	April - June	6	21 - 35 days
Antirrhinum	July - September	6	10 - 14 days
Aster	April - May	12	10 - 14 days
Calendula	March - May	12	10 - 14 days
Candytuft	May - July	6	10 - 14 days
Dahlia	May - June	6	10 - 14 days
Daisy	May - June	6	10 - 14 days
Delphinium	May - June	6	14 - 21 days
Freesia	March - June	12	21 - 28 days
Hollyhock	May - June	12	14 - 21 days
Lupin	April - June	12.	21 - 28 days
Marigold	May - June	6	7 - 10 days
Nasturtium	April - May	12	10 - 14 days
Pansy	June - July	6	14 - 28 days
Petunia	May - June	3	7 - 14 days
Poppy	March - May	6	10 - 14 days
Stock	April	6	7 - 10 days

Paper: Suitable.

SLIMMERS!
WATCH YOUR CARBOHYDRATES
(Average person maximum of 50 grams)

Food	Quantity	grams
Apple pie	Slice	55
Banana	1	35
Biscuit: chocolate	1	7
plain	1	8
Bread	Slice	13
Cake: fruit	Slice	25
Sponge	Slice	25
Fried potatoes	5	10
Ice cream: vanilla	cup	14
chocolate	cup	16
Sundae	portion	56
Orange	1	20
Pancake	1	40
Peach	1	12
Peas: fresh	portion	12
tinned	portion	30
Pear	1	27
Plums: fresh	1	10
tinned	small tin	55
Potatoes: boiled	1	25
roasted	1	30

Paper: Suitable. Rule up if your teacher asks you
to do so.

WASHING INSTRUCTIONS
FOR MACHINES

Fabric	°C	Notes
Cotton, Linen (white)	95	Maximum wash, long spin
Cotton, Linen (coloured)	90	Maximum wash, long spin
Nylon, Polyester/cotton (white)	60	Medium wash, short spin
Nylon, Polyester/cotton (coloured)	50	Medium wash, short spin
Acrylics; Acetates and Triacetates including mixtures with wool	40	Medium wash, short spin
Wool	40	Medium wash, short spin
Silk and printed Acetate fabrics with colours not fast	30	Minimum wash, short spin

Check the article label for items which
cannot be washed - see if they are to be
dry cleaned.

Paper: A5 (210 × 148 mm).

COMPOUND INTEREST

Sum to which each unit will amount each year

Years	2½%	3%	4%	5%
1	1·025	1·030	1·040	1·050
2	1·050	1·060	1·080	1·102
3	1·077	1·093	1·123	1·158
4	1·104	1·126	1·170	1·215
5	1·131	1·160	1·217	1·277
6	1·160	1·194	1·265	1·340
7	1·189	1·230	1·316	1·407
8	1·218	1·267	1·369	1·447
9	1·249	1·305	1·423	1·551
10	1·280	1·344	1·480	1·629

Figures to third decimal point.

Paper: A5 (210 x 148 mm).

IDEAL WEIGHTS FOR WOMEN
(in stones and pounds)

Height	Slim build		Medium Build		Large Build	
4ft 8ins	6	11	7	4	8	0
4ft 9ins	7	0	7	6	8	2
4ft 10ins	7	2	7	9	8	5
4ft 11ins	7	5	7	13	8	9
5ft 0ins	7	9	8	0	8	12
5ft 1ins	7	11	8	5	9	1
5ft 2ins	7	14	8	9	9	5
5ft 3ins	8	2	8	13	9	10
5ft 4ins	8	7	9	1	9	14
5ft 5ins	8	12	9	7	10	1
5ft 6ins	9	0	9	13	10	5
5ft 7ins	9	6	10	1	10	11

Paper: Suitable.   Arrange the composers into chronological order in 2 columns.

COMPOSERS OF CLASSICAL MUSIC

Composer	Born	Composer	Born	Composer	Born
Albinoni	1671	Chopin	1810	Mahler	1860
Balakireff	1837	Cimarosa	1749	Mozart	1756
Bax	1883	Copland	1900	Nielsen	1865
Beethoven	1770	Corelli	1653	Prokofiev	1891
Berg	1885	Debussy	1862	Purcell	1658
Berlioz	1803	Dukas	1865	Ravel	1875
Boccherini	1743	Elgar	1857	Rossini	1792
Brahms	1833	Glinka	1804	Schubert	1797
Byrd	1542	Handel	1685	Smetana	1824
Cesti	1623	Haydn	1732	Weber	1786

Paper: Suitable. Type the following in alphabetical order in 3 columns headed
ROADS   STREETS   LANES
Do not type ROAD, STREET or LANE after each name.

Meadow Lane
Windsor Road
Calshill Road
Pass Street
Cairns Street
Victoria Street
Oaken Lane
Church Road
Benton Street
Charles Lane
Woodside Lane

North Street
Gower Street
Rookery Lane
Peake Road
Hunter Street
Market Street
Marsh Lane
Tanfield Road
Egerton Road
Haley Street
Kingfisher Lane

Moore Road
Dartford Street
Coppice Lane
Station Road
Sandyfields Lane
Springfield Road
Keepers Lane
Charles Road
Priory Street
Neath Street
West Lane

Church Road
Tudor Lane
Watling Street
Dursley Road
Norbury Road
Clifton Lane
Weston Street
Hall Lane
Poplar Road
Caswell Road
Fairfield Lane
Beech Street

41

Paper: Suitable. Rule up if your teacher asks you to do so.

COMPOSITION OF THE HUMAN BODY

Element	%	Use
Oxygen	65.00	Blood. Most other compounds.
Carbon	18.60	Bi-carbonates, carbohydrates, fats and proteins.
Hydrogen	9.50	Carbohydrates, fats and proteins.
Nitrogen	3.40	Found in proteins.
Calcium	1.50	Bones and teeth.
Phosphorus	1.00	Bones and teeth. Energy generating compounds.
Potassium	0.30	Blood and body fluids.
Sulphur	0.30	Found in some proteins.
Chlorine	0.20	Body fluids.
Sodium	0.16	Blood and body fluids.
Magnesium	0.05	Bone, brain and nerve cells.
Iron	Minute	Red blood cells.
Iodine	Minute	Hormones
Cobalt	Minute	Essential for blood formation.
Manganese	Minute	Helps control cell chemistry.
Copper	Minute	Part of blood cells.
Fluorine	Minute	Found in teeth.

Paper: Suitable. Arrange the students into alphabetical order. Type surnames first and type them in capital letters. The main heading is EXAMINATION RESULTS. Rule up if your teacher asks you to do so.

Student	Typewriting	Shorthand	Office Practice
Muriel Rosillo	75	80	72
Joy Quist	80	71	76
Elizabeth Vokes	70	90	80
Sandra Mugwagwa	91	89	79
Vivien De Burgo	77	83	78
Jean Odaantjis	94	88	96
Anne Dando	59	62	84
Jill Ziegler	71	84	45
Juliana Uhart	97	91	96
Doris Rosee	66	40	75
Sonia Prantl	50	72	91

Paper: Suitable. Type the following in 4 columns headed <u>Mice</u> <u>Rabbits</u> <u>Rats</u> <u>Shrews</u>. The main heading is SPECIES ILLUSTRATED. Mice are indicated (M), Rabbits (Ra), Rats (Rt) and Shrews (S). Type each species in alphabetical order.

Musk (s)	Briar (Ra)	African Giant (Rt)
Fish-eating (Rt)	True (Ra)	Forest (Ra)
Harvest (M)	Lesser Cane (Rt)	House (M)
Bamboo (Rt)	Armoured (s)	Molly (Ra)
Cottontail (Ra)	Allen's Cotton (Ra)	African Tree (M)
Elephant (s)	Pine (M)	Mexican Pigmy (Ra)
Hero (s)	Indian House (s)	Coffee (Rt)
Kusu (Rt)	Trade (Rt)	European (s)
Meadow (M)	Norway (Rt)	Idaho Pigmy (Ra)
Lemming (M)	Snow (M)	Red-backed (M)
American Water (s)	Etruscan (s)	
Swamp (Ra)	Masked (s)	
Water (Rt)	Dwarf (M)	
Otter (s)	Sumatra (Ra)	
Scorpion (m)	Rice (Rt)	

Paper: Suitable.   Type the following in alphabetical order in 3 columns headed
SINGLE   DOUBLE   SEMI-DOUBLE.   The main heading is FUCHSIAS.   Single are indicated
by (S), Double by (D) and Semi-double by (SD).   Type each type in alphabetical
order.

Kathleen (D)	Alaska (D)	Festival (SD)
Phyllis (SD)	Amigo (SD)	Icicle (D)
Margaret (SD)	Butterfly (S)	Leonora (S)
Flash (S)	Caesar (D)	Icecap (S)
Lena (S)	Barbara (S)	Melody (S)
Trase (D)	Circe (SD)	Mandarin (SD)
Vulcan (SD)	Festival (S)	Newhope (D)
Esther (D)	Heritage (SD)	Martina (S)
Tumbler (SD)	Gala (D)	Rosebud (D)
Anne (S)	Flora (SD)	Rahnee (D)
Antonia (S)	Hombre (D)	Robin (D)
		Streamliner (SD)
		Scarlet (SD)
		Snowdrift (SD)
		Temptation (S)
		Sonata (D)
		Ruffles (D)
		Plenty (S)
		Pantaloons (SD)
		Muriel (SD)
		Masquerade (D)
		Bouffant (S)
		Beacon (S)

45

Paper: Suitable. Display the following in 3
columns headed <u>Floribunda</u>   <u>Hybrid Tea</u>   <u>Polyantha</u>
in alphabetical order. The main heading is
<u>ROSES CURRENTLY AVAILABLE</u>. Floribunda roses are
indicated by (F), Hybrid Tea by (H) and Polyantha
by (P).

Sunshine (P)

Orange Silk (F)

Cameo (P)

Dimples (F)

Coral Star (H)

Summer Holiday (H)

Baby Betty (P)

Allgold (F)

Golden Salmon (P)

Margaret (H)

Gold Crown (H)

Zambra (F)

Baby Sylvia (P)

Cri Cri (P)

Tip Top (F)

Arakan (F)

Blue Moon (H)

Masquerade (F)

Lady Seton (H)

The Fairy (P)

Fairy Dancers (H)

Lady Sylvia (H)

Iceberg (F)

Baby Sylvia (F)

Golden Treasure (F)

Ideal (P)

My Choice (H)

Fresh Pink (P)

Pink Peace (H)

Coral Cluster (P)

Paper: Suitable.   Arrange the places into
alphabetical order.

THE WEATHER

Around the World

	°C	°F
NICE	14	57
Helsinki	8	46
Vienna	4	39
Moscow	12	54
Algiers	12	54
Istanbul	12	54
Vancouver	8	46
Paris	8	46
Barcelona	11	52
Tangier	14	57
New York	18	64
Malta	21	70
Tel-Aviv	19	66
Rome	20	68
Warsaw	6	43
Geneva	6	43
Casablanca	16	61
Athens	17	63
Copenhagen	6	43
Oporto	11	52
Las Palmas	18	64

Paper: Suitable. Use leader dots if you wish.

SALES ABROAD

	1979	%	1978	%
Europe	564	19	330	18
North America	314	11	183	10
Africa	255	9	155	9
Australasia	154	5	103	5
Near East	136	5	78	4
India and Pakistan	83	3	48	3
South and Central America	37	1	27	1
Far East	36	1	26	1
	1579	100	948	100

Paper: A5 (210 x 148 mm). Display - use leader
dots if you wish.

COMPOSITION OF THE EARTH'S ATMOSPHERE

Gas	%
Nitrogen	78.0000
Oxygen	21.0000
Argon	0.9400
Carbon dioxide	0.0300
Hydrogen	0.0100
Neon	0.0012
Helium	0.0004
Water vapour	Variable

Paper: A5 (210 x 148 mm). Display - use leader
dots if you wish.

CONTENTS

	Page
Preface	5
The earth's atmosphere	15
The earth's crust	75
Land forms	126
Lakes	219
Seas and oceans	329
Vegetation	470
Rivers	221

Paper: Suitable.   Arrange the stands into
numerical order.

CAREERS   EXHIBITION

Stand No.	Career Topic	Sessions
23	Accountancy	All
22	Architecture	1 and 3
20	Army and WAC	All
1 and 2	Careers Service	All
21	Computer Work	1, 2, 4, 5
11 and 12	Construction	All
16	Electrical Work	All
17	Engineering	All
5	Engineering	All
3	Engineering	All
19	Fire Service	All
4	Gas Industry	2, 3, 5, 6
10	Journalism	2
13	Leatherwork	All
7	Merchant Navy	3 and 6
15	Motor Vehicle Maintenance	All
6	Police	All
8	Air Force and WAF	All
18	Navy, Marines WNS	All
9	Telecommunications	All
14	Building Society Work	All
15	Civil Service	2, 3, 5, 6
21	Photography	All
24 and 25	Hospital Services	All

Paper: Suitable. Display the towns in rank order -
starting with the largest.

SOME OF THE WORLD'S LARGEST TOWNS

Town	Country	Population (000.)
Shanghai	China	10820
Rangoon	Burma	3187
Paris	France	9108
Calcutta	India	7005
Kingston	Jamaica	573
Bombay	India	5970
Sydney	Australia	2874
Vienna	Austria	1860
Montréal	Canada	2775
Oslo	Norway	469
Lagos	Nigeria	1500
Kampala	Uganda	330
Tokyo	Japan	11670
Nairobi	Kenya	630
Greater London	England	7169
New York	USA	11572
Los Angeles	USA	7033
Birmingham	England	1004
Cardiff	Wales	277
Glasgow	Scotland	817
Belfast	Northern Ireland	374

Paper: Suitable. Display the following information
to best advantage on one sheet of paper - folded if
you wish.

CLOTHING SIZES

WOMEN'S

Dresses

British	French	American
32/8	38	
34/10	40	
36/12	42	10
38/14	44	
40/16	46	16
42/18	48	

Blouses

British	American	Continental
34	32	46
36	34	42
38	36	44
40	38	46
42	40	48
44	42	50

MEN'S

Shirts

British	American	Continental
13	13	33
14	14	35-36
15	15	38
16	16	40-41
17	17	43

Suits

British	American	Continental
36	36	34
38	38	36
40	40	38
42	42	40
44	44	42

WOMEN'S SHOES

British	American	Continental
3	5	34
4	6	36
5	7	38
6	8	40
7	9	42

MEN'S SHOES

British	American	Continental
7	7	40.5
8	8	42.0
9	9	43.0
10	10	44.5
11	11	45.0

Paper: Suitable. Type the following in numerical order - starting with the smallest number of calories.

CALORIE CHART

Food	Calories	Food	Calories
Bread-White	73	Apple	12
Bread-Brown	68	Apricot	14
Bread-Wholemeal	66	Banana	21
Rice	99	Gooseberries	5
Egg	45	Grapefruit	6
Lard	253	Orange	10
Margarine	218	Strawberries	7
Bacon	128	Raisins	67
Beef	75	Lettuce	3
Chicken	38	Peas	17
Mutton	94	Beans-French	4
Pork	115	Sugar	108
Sausage-pork	97	Honey	78
Sausage-beef	72	Coffee-ground	0
Kippers	62	Cocoa-powder	125
Cod	19	Tea	0
Herring	55	Cabbage	7

All values are for an ounce of raw food

Paper: Suitable. Arrange the countries into alphabetical order.

EXCHANGE RATES

as at 19 April

Country	Currency	Rate
Jamaica	US $*	1.71
Bahamas	US $*	1.71
Egypt	Egyptian Pound	1.21
United States	US $	1.71
Singapore	Singapore $	4.23
Antigua	US $*	1.71
Kenya	Kenya Shilling	14.23
Seychelles	Rupees	13.93
Mauritius	Rupees	11.40
Bermuda	US $*	1.71
Thailand	Baht	34.97
India	Rupees	15.13
Sierre Leone	Leones	2.00
Malaysia	Ringgits	4.28

* These countries have their own units of currency but prices relate to US $

Paper: A4. Leave 25 mm blank at the head of the page. Draw a rectangle 150 x 100 mm to represent diagrams of a car. Display to best advantage.

DIMENSIONS

		in	cm
Front seat head room	A	35.37	89.86
Rear seat head room	B	31.65	80.39
Front seat cushion depth	C	19.05	48.95
Rear seat cushion depth	D	18.45	46.05
Front seat height	E	22.15	56.35
Rear seat height	F	21.05	53.55
Distance between seats - maximum	G	17.00	42.40
Distance between seats - minimum	H	9.00	23.50
Steering wheel to front seat - maximum	I	18.50	47.00
Steering wheel to front seat - minimum	J	13.00	33.00
Luggage boot height	K	20.00	50.50
Luggage boot depth	L	40.50	102.70
Luggage boot width	M	39.00	99.50
Front cushions overall width	N	48.00	121.50
Rear cushions overall width	O	54.00	135.50
Width between front doors	P	54.00	135.50
Overall height - maximum	Q	55.00	137.50
Overall width	R	68.00	172.50
Overall length	S	176.00	440.00
Kerbside weight (approximate)	T	2210 lb	995 kg

Paper: Suitable. Insert leader dots if you wish. Arrange the Index into alphabetical order.

CLASSIFIED ADVERTISEMENT INDEX

Holidays: Home	23-26
Abroad	21-23
Afloat	26-28
Accommodation	23
Motors	43-50
Concerts	10
Art Galleries	8
TV and Radio	30
Property: Home	41-43
Abroad	38-41
Exhibitions	18
Mortgages	35
Business opportunities	20
Personal	51
Cinema	32
Educational courses	19-20
Theatres	33
Appointments: Educational ..	51-53
Universities ..	55-58
Public ..	53-55
Social Services ..	58-61
Gardening	19
Mini market	62-63

Paper: A5 (210 x 148 mm).
Use leader dots if you wish.

ATLANTIS TRUST COMPANY LIMITED

Portfolio Distribution

	1979 %	1978 %
Africa	43.6	33.8
USA and Canada	32.9	30.7
Japan and Far East	3.9	6.1
Europe	1.2	2.7
South America	1.0	1.8
Fixed Interest	8.0	5.0
Cash and short-term deposits	9.4	19.9
	100.0	100.0

Paper: A5 (210 x 148 mm).
Use leader dots if you wish.

ATLANTIS TRUST COMPANY LIMITED

CONTENTS

Notice of meeting	1
Financial Highlights	2
Directors	3
Chairman's Statement	4-7
Operating Review	8-15
Report of the Directors	16-20
Profit and Loss Account	21
Balance Sheet	22
Notes to the Accounts	23-30
Report of the Auditors	31-33

Paper: Suitable.

EQUIVALENTS OF SIZES

Size	Metric size (mm)	Imperial size (inches)
A1	595 × 840	23 × 33
SRA2	450 × 640	$17\frac{1}{2} \times 25$
RA2	430 × 610	17 × 24
Royal	520 × 635	$20\frac{1}{2} \times 25$
Demy	445 × 570	$17\frac{1}{2} \times 22\frac{1}{4}$
A2	420 × 595	$16\frac{1}{2} \times 23\frac{1}{2}$
A3	420 × 297	$16\frac{1}{2} \times 11\frac{3}{4}$
Brief	406 × 330	16 × 13
Foolscap	330 × 203	13 × 8
A4	297 × 210	$11\frac{3}{4} \times 8\frac{1}{4}$
Quarto	254 × 203	10 × 8
$\frac{2}{3}$ A4	210 × 197	$8\frac{1}{4} \times 7\frac{7}{8}$
Sixmo	203 × 178	8 × 7
A5	210 × 148	$8\frac{1}{4} \times 5\frac{7}{8}$

Paper: Suitable. Use leader dots if you wish.

PRESIDENTS OF THE UNITED STATES

President	Party	Term
George Washington	Federal	1789-1797
John Adams	Federal	1797-1801
Thomas Jefferson	Republican	1801-1809
James Madison	Republican	1809-1817
James Monroe	Republican	1817-1825
John Quincey Adams	Republican	1825-1829
Andrew Jackson	Democratic	1829-1837
Martin Van Buren	Democratic	1837-1841
William Harrison	Whig	1841 (died)
John Tyler	Whig	1841-1845
James Polk	Democratic	1845-1849
Zachery Taylor	Whig	1849-1850 (died)
Millard Fullmore	Whig	1850-1853
Franklin Pierce	Democratic	1853-1857
James Buchanan	Democratic	1857-1861
Abraham Lincoln	Republican	1861-1865 (assassinated)
Andrew Johnson	Republican	1865-1869
Ulysses S Grant	Republican	1869-1877
Rutherford B Hayes	Republican	1877-1881
James A Garfield	Republican	1881 (assassinated)
Chester A Arthur	Republican	1881-1885
Grover Cleveland	Democratic	1885-1889
Benjamin Harrison	Republican	1889-1893
Grover Cleveland	Democratic	1893-1897

Paper: Suitable. Use leader dots if you wish.

INDEX

Subject	Month	Page
Annual economic review ...	April	2
Balance of payments	August	10
Cars and motoring	February	15
Company income	April	26
Economic policy	November	34
Economic review	April	42
Exports	June	54
Financial information	November	62
Household spending	August	74
Income	June	86
Industry	December	97
Inflation	June	103
Imports	August	112
Macro-economic model	April	136
Overseas earnings	November	144
Public expenditure	July	157
Reserves	May	172

Paper: Suitable. Display to best advantage.

<u>BANKING CONVERSION COURSES</u>

<u>Part-time day</u>

Economics
Principles of law } Tuesday 0900 – 1700
Accounting

Economics
Principles of law } Wednesday 0900 – 1700
Accounting

<u>Evenings only</u>

Principles of Law) Monday 1830 – 2030
Accounting } Wednesday 1830 – 2030
Economics) Friday 1830 – 2030

Paper: Suitable. Display to best advantage.

<u>DIPLOMA IN SALES MANAGEMENT</u>

Section B   Personnel Control
Time Control } Monday 1800 – 2000

C   Policy Control
Cost Control } Monday 2000 – 2130

D   Communication Control)
Advertising and Marketing } Wednesday 1800 – 2000
Research)

A   Legal Control
Statistical Control } Friday 2000 – 2130

Paper: A5 (210 × 148 mm).

CERTIFICATE IN MANAGEMENT PRINCIPLES

Part A

Personnel Management
Accounting and Statistics
Economics
      Monday   0900-1700

Part B

Law
Marketing and Merchandising
Fundamentals of Distribution
Project/Essay
      Wednesday   0900-1700

Supplementary Studies

Distribution
Computers in Management
Statistics of Distribution
      Tuesday   1800-1900
                        1900-2000
                        2000-2100

Paper: Suitable.
Type the metals in alphabetical order.

METALS

Symbols and atomic weights

Metal	Symbol	Atomic weight
Gold	Au	196.97
Silver	Ag	107.87
Copper	Cu	63.54
Tin	Sn	118.69
Lead	Pb	207.19
Titanium	Ti	47.90
Magnesium	Mg	24.31
Calcium	Ca	40.08
Aluminium	Al	26.98
Sodium	Na	22.99
Mercury	Hg	200.59
Chromium	Cr	52.00
Platinum	Pt	195.09
Tungsten	W	183.85

Paper: Suitable.

TYPING COURSE

Day	Date	Time	Room
Tuesday	28 June	1000-1200	816
Wednesday	29 June	0930-1200	818
Thursday	30 June	0930-1200	816
Monday	4 July	1000-1200	818
		1330-1600	816
Tuesday	5 July	1000-1200	818
Wednesday	6 July	0930-1200	818
Thursday	7 July	0930-1200	818
Monday	11 July	1000-1200	816
		1330-1600	818
Tuesday	12 July	1000-1200	818
Wednesday	13 July	0930-1200	818
Thursday	14 July	0930-1200	818
Monday	18 July	1000-1200	816
		1330-1600	818
Tuesday	19 July	1000-1200	818
Wednesday	20 July	0930-1230	818
Thursday	21 July	1000-1200	818

Paper: Suitable.

HOLIDAYS FAR AND WIDE

Resort	Hotel	Peak Season	Low Season
SEYCHELLES	Northolme Reef	December to August	August to December
BERMUDA	Belmont Colony Club	March to October	October to March
BANGKOK	New Amarin Indra Regent	December to January	March to October
NAIROBI	Serena Safari Park	November to December	September to November
SLIEMA	Ideal Gzira	July to August	April to May
GIBRALTAR	Rock Queens	July to August	April to May
SALOU	Augustus Cala Font	July to August	April and October
MALLIA	Belvedere Nora	July to August	March and October

Typist! Arrange the resorts in alphabetical order.

Paper: Suitable. Arrange the countries into alphabetical order.

COUNTRIES
THEIR CAPITALS, CURRENCIES AND LANGUAGES

COUNTRY	CAPITAL	CURRENCY	LANGUAGE
Czechoslavakia	Prague	Koruna	Czech/Slovak
Canada	Ottawa	Dollar	French/English
Denmark	Copenhagen	Krone	Danish
Peru	Lima	Sol	Spanish
Japan	Tokyo	Yen	Japenese
Greece	Athens	Dvachma	Greek
Turkey	Istanbul	Lira	Turkish
Italy	Rome	Lire	Italian
Austria	Vienna	Schilling	German
Brazil	Brazilia	Cruzeiro	Portuguese
Sudan	Khartoum	Pound	Arabic
Kenya	Nairobi	Shilling	Swahili
Nigeria	Lagos	Pound	Many local dialects
Spain	Madrid	Peseta	Spanish
France	Paris	Francs	French
England	London	Pound	English

Paper: Suitable.

PART-TIME EVENING COURSES

Course Number	Subject	Day	Time
First Year			
510	History	Thursday	1900-2100
512	Economics	Tuesday	1900-2100
513	Geography	Monday	1900-2130
514	French	Wednesday	1830-2030
515	Sociology	Friday	1900-2100
516	Government	Tuesday	1845-2115
Second Year			
520	History	Tuesday	1900-2100
522	Economics	Thursday	1900-2100
523	Geography	Friday	1900-2130
524	French	Monday	1830-2030
525	Sociology	Wednesday	1900-2100
526	Government	Friday	1845-2115
Third Year			
530	History	Monday	1900-2100
532	Economics	Friday	1900-2100
533	Geography	Wednesday	1900-2130
534	French	Thursday	1830-2030
535	Sociology	Monday	1900-2100
536	Government	Thursday	1845-2115

Paper: Suitable.

DIMENSIONS

EXTERIOR

Overall length	140.8 ins	3568 mm
Overall height	52.0 ins	1317 mm
Maximum width	62.0 ins	1570 mm
Wheelbase	90.5 ins	2290 mm
Front track	52.8 ins	1339 mm
Rear track	52.5 ins	1334 mm

INTERIOR

Front headroom	38.0 ins	960 mm
Front legroom	40.5 ins	1025 mm
Front shoulder room	50.5 ins	1282 mm
Front hiproom	50.5 ins	1282 mm
Rear headroom	37.0 ins	939 mm
Rear legroom	34.5 ins	881 mm
Rear shoulder room	50.5 ins	1282 mm
Rear hiproom	50.5 ins	1282 mm

Paper: Suitable. Type the following in rank order - starting with the largest.

Name	Area (Square Miles)	Average Depth*	Greatest Depth*
Caribbean Sea	750 000	8 405	23 755
North Sea	221 000	180	2 166
Atlantic Ocean	31 529 000	12 881	27 515
Yellow Sea	480 000	162	350
Red Sea	178 000	1 491	9 300
Pacific Ocean	63 985 000	14 042	37 780
Baltic Sea	158 000	220	1 400
Indian Ocean	28 357 000	13 000	24 480
Bering Sea	878 000	1 666	13 425
Mediterranean Sea	1 145 000	4 500	15 705
Black Sea	168 000	4 300	7 365
Arctic Sea	5 540 000	4 200	17 500

* In feet

70

Paper: Suitable. Arrange the rivers in order of length – starting with the largest.

SOME OF THE WORLD'S MAJOR RIVERS

Name	Outflow	Length (miles)
Lena	Arctic Sea	2,800
Congo	Atlantic	3,000
Yukon	Bering Sea	2,000
Amazon	Atlantic	4,050
Volga	Caspian Sea	2,400
Mississippi-Missouri	Gulf of Mexico	3,760
St. Lawrence	Gulf of St. Lawrence	1,800
Mekong	China Sea	2,800
Colorado	Gulf of California	2,000
Nile	Mediterranean	4,160
Yangtse	North Pacific	3,400
Yenisei	Arctic Sea	3,300
Ob	Arctic Sea	2,700

Paper: Suitable. Type the mountains in alphabetical order.

SOME OF THE WORLD'S MAJOR MOUNTAINS

Name	Range	Height (feet)
Everest	Himalayas	29,030
Godwin-Austen (K2)	Karakoram	28,252
Kanchenjunga	Himalayas	28,150
Nanga Parbat	Himalayas	26,630
Nanda Devi	Himalayas	25,600
Kamet	Himalayas	25,450
Minya Konka	China	24,900
Aconcagua	Andes	22,835

Paper: Suitable.

THE WORLD'S LARGEST LAKES

Name	Location	Area (sq miles)
Caspian Sea	Asia	170 000
Superior	North America	31 821
Victoria	Africa	26 204
Aral	USSR	24 399
Huron	North America	23 000
Michigan	North America	22 425
Malawi	Africa	14 220
Tanganyika	Africa	12 650
Great Bear	Canada	11 666
Baikal	USSR	11 585
Great Slave	Canada	11 175

Paper: Suitable.

WEIGHTS AND TOWING LIMITS

Model	Engine	Kerb weight		Towing limit (2-up)	
Pacific	958cc	1544 lbs	700kg	1250 lbs	566kg
Pacific S	958cc	1580 lbs	720kg	1200 lbs	546kg
Pacific	1120cc	1580 lbs	720kg	1770 lbs	820kg
Pacific S	1120cc	1600 lbs	735kg	1770 lbs	820kg
Pacific GS	958cc	1610 lbs	750kg	1200 lbs	549kg
Pacific GS	1120cc	1610 lbs	750kg	1770 lbs	820kg

Paper: Suitable.

STRUCTURE OF MANUFACTURING INDUSTRY

Sector	Employment	Exports	Imports
Food	11.0	9.3	12.0
Drink	1.9	0.6	2.2
Tobacco	0.5	0.1	0.1
Textiles, clothing	28.6	30.0	5.0
Wood and cork	5.0	10.8	0.6
Furniture	5.1	1.1	0.1
Pulp	0.5	5.5	0.4
Paper and board	2.2	2.0	1.0
Printing	1.0	0.9	0.5
Tanning, footwear	5.3	2.0	1.0
Rubber	0.1	0.8	0.4
Chemicals	5.7	8.0	0.5
Fertilisers	0.5	2.4	15.0
Oil and coal	0.5	2.0	0.4
Non-metallic minerals	6.0	3.0	3.0
Cement	2.9	0.2	2.2
Basic metals	1.9	1.7	0.1
Metal products	6.1	2.0	11.1
Non-electric machines	1.2	2.0	3.0
Electrical equipment	5.0	4.0	16.4
Shipbuilding	5.9	8.7	8.0
Transport	3.1	2.9	14.0
Total	100.0	100.0	100.0

Paper: Suitable.

BY COACH FROM LONDON TO PARIS

Using Hovercraft

1 March to 21 March

London Depart	Ramsgate Depart	Calais Arrive	Paris Arrive	Flight Number
0800	1045	1230	1715	105
1000	1245	1430	1915	116
1300	1545	1730	2215	109

22 March to 2 June

1000	1245	1325	1815	106
1030	1315	1355	1845	117
1145	1715	1755	2035	110

3 June to 14 July

0800	1045	1230	1715	205
1000	1245	1430	1915	216
1300	1545	1730	2215	209

Paper: A5 (210 x 148 mm).

red	orange	black
yellow	gold	white
green	grey	silver
blue	bronze	pink

Retype the above in alphabetical order.

Paper: A5 (210 x 148 mm).

pansy	snapdragon	cosmea
lupin	rose	foxglove
verbena	petunia	carnation
pink	phlox	alyssum
lily	primrose	aster
nigella	daisy	flax

Retype the above in alphabetical order.

Paper: A5 (210 x 148 mm).

CARS

Austin	Aston Martin	Ford
B M W	Jeep	Mazda
Alfa Romeo	Porsche	Mercedes-Benz
Chevrolet	Vauxhall	Skoda
Jaguar	Subaru	Triumph
Renault	Lada	Fiat
Volkswagen	Datsun	Matra-Simica

Retype in alphabetical order.

Paper: A5 (210 x 148 mm).

OFFICE EQUIPMENT

dictation machine	storage unit	photo-copier
typewriter	paper clip	folding machine
telephone	file	
addressing machine	computer	copyholder
	Spirit-duplicator	desk
punch		chair
stapler	collating machine	cash box

Retype in alphabetical order.

Paper: Suitable. Type the Battles as they are. Retype in alphabetical order.
Retype in date order – starting with the earliest.

FAMOUS BATTLES

Almanza	1707	Sevastopol	1855	Legnano	1176
Valmy	1792	Sadowa	1866	Agincourt	1415
Panipat	1761	Nile	1798	Chioggia	1380
Navarino	1827	Quebec	1759	Nancy	1477
Saratoga	1777	Lepanto	1571	Poitiers	1356
Verdun	1916	Edgehill	1642	Pavia	1525
Tsushima	1905	Fehrbellin	1675	Majuba	1881
Sedan	1870	Chaldiran	1514	Woerth	1870

Paper: A5 (210 x 148 mm).

Canada	India
Toronto	Agra
Vancouver	Bombay
Calgary	Calcutta
Regina	Hyderabad
Winnipeg	Kanpur

Paper: A5 (210 x 148 mm).

Italy	Japan	Nigeria
Bologna	Chiba	Abeokuta
Milano	Nagasaki	Lagos
Napoli	Osaka	Maiduguri
Rimini	Yokohama	Ogbomosho

Paper: Suitable. Arrange the Bridges and Tunnels into alphabetical order.

The Longest Bridges	The Longest Railway Tunnels
Sydney Harbour	Severn
Severn	Sodbury
Upper Sone	Oxted
Golden Gate	Box
Tay Road Bridge	Kilsby
Hardinge	Mersey
Rio Dulce	Halton
Godavari	Caerphilly

Paper: A5 (210 x 148 mm).

Some White Wines	Some Red Wines
Barsac	Arsac
Chablis	Labarde
Pouilly	Margaux
Sauternes	Pauillac

Paper: A5 (210 x 148 mm).

European Towns	African Towns	American Towns
Agen	Dakar	Albany
Bologna	Kampala	Clayton
Leipzig	Nairobi	Denver
Namur	Nyala	Pierre
Padua	Sarh	Waco

Paper: A5 (210 x 148 mm).

RECOMMENDED INTEREST RATES

Month of Recommendation	Net Share Rate %	Mortgage Rate %
September 1976	7.80	12.25
March 1977	7.00	11.25
July 1977	6.50	10.50
October 1977	6.00	9.50
February 1978	5.50	8.50

Paper: A5 (210 x 148 mm).

PRIMARY SI UNITS

Length	metre	m
Mass	kilogramme	kg
Time	Second	s
Electrical current	ampere	A
Temperature	kelvin	k
Luminous intensity	Candela	cd

Paper: Suitable.

LANGUAGE CLASSES

Every evening, 1900 - 2100, as follows:-

Language	Monday	Tuesday	Wednesday	Thursday	Friday
French	Grade I	Grade II	Grade I	Grade II	Grade III
German	Grade III	Grade I	Grade III		Grade I
Spanish	Grade II		Grade II	Grade I	
Italian	Grade III		Grade II		Grade I
Russian		Grade I	Grade II	Grade III	
Esperanto	Grade I	Grade III			Grade II

Paper: Suitable.

TIMETABLE

Valid from 25 April to 29 September

Sailing Period	From Felixstowe	From Newcastle	From Gothenburg
25 April - 28 May	Monday Friday	Saturday Sunday	
28 May - 29 June	Monday Saturday Sunday	Wednesday Saturday Sunday	Friday to Felixstowe Saturday to Newcastle
29 June - 30 August	Monday Saturday Sunday	Wednesday Saturday Sunday	Thursday to Newcastle Friday to Felixstowe Saturday to Newcastle Sunday to Felixstowe
31 August - 29 September	Monday	Saturday	Friday to Felixstowe Saturday to Newcastle

Paper: Suitable. Display and rule up.

CALENDAR MONTHLY REPAYMENTS (8.5% interest)

Amount of Advance	35 Years	30 Years	Amount of Advance	25 Years	20 Years
£	£	£	£	£	£
25	0.20	0.20	25	0.26	0.30
50	0.40	0.40	50	0.40	0.50
100	0.80	0.80	100	0.90	0.90
200	1.50	1.60	200	1.70	1.80
300	2.30	2.40	300	2.50	2.70
400	3.00	3.10	400	3.30	3.60
500	3.80	3.90	500	4.10	4.40
1000	7.60	7.80	1000	8.20	8.80
2000	15.10	15.60	2000	16.30	17.70
3000	22.60	23.30	3000	24.50	26.50
4000	30.10	31.10	4000	32.60	35.30
5000	37.60	38.80	5000	40.80	44.10

Paper: Suitable.

RULED PAPER

Sheet Size	Ruling	Unpunched Reference	Punched Reference
Foolscap	Feint	122	122 P
	Feint and Margin	122 M	122 PM
	Narrow Feint	119	119 P
	Plain	100	100 P
A4	Feint	231	231 P
	Feint and Margin	231 M	231 PM
	Narrow Feint	240	240 P
	Plain	250	250 P
	Plain and Margin	260 M	260 PM
Quarto	Feint	300	300 P
	Feint and Margin	301 M	301 PM
	Narrow Feint	302	302 P
	Plain	310	310 P
	Plain and Margin	320 M	320 PM

Paper: Suitable.

NUMBER OF PERSONS MIGRATING.

Year	From North to South	From South to North	From West to East	From East to West
1972	73140	19525	14710	13621
1973	25726	43629	16001	13661
1974	19472	18987	3526	6421
1975	11005	15123	3627	6229
1976	10856	12978	4927	2491
1977	13792	13626	9421	6228

Paper: Suitable.

10 VARIETIES OF APPLES

Variety (c indicates cookers)	Week for picking	Season of use	Colour	Comments
George Cave	August - 2nd	Mid-August	Green/yellow	Crisp, juicy, small core
Grenadier (c)	August - 2nd	August - September	Light green	Does not store well
James Grieve	September - 2nd	September - October	Yellow/red flush	Susceptable to apple canker
George Neal (c)	August - 3rd	August - October	Yellow/orange flush	Good quality
Sunset	September - 4th	November - December	Golden yellow	Fine flavour
Cox's Orange Pippin	October - 1st	November - December	Yellow/dark red	Fine flavour
Bramley's Seedling (c)	October - 2nd	November - February	Yellow/red flush	The finest cooking apple
Golden Delicious	October - 3rd	November - January	Yellow	Easy to grow
Crispin	October - 3rd	December - February	Yellow	Heavy cropper
Annie Elizabeth (c)	October - 3rd	December - June	Green/red	Grows well in the North

Paper: Suitable.

House Purchase
By Mortgage
(interest at 9.5% over 30 years)

House Price	Deposit (minimum)	Sum Borrowed	Weekly Income Required	Monthly Repayment *
10,000	500	9,500	68.00	58.81
11,000	550	10,450	73.00	64.69
12,000	600	11,400	80.00	70.57
13,000	650	12,350	85.00	75.83
14,000	700	13,300	91.00	82.33
15,000	750	14,250	97.00	88.20

* This excludes Life and Property insurance

Paper: Suitable. Use leader dots if you wish.

GUIDE TO OIL TEMPERATURES

Food	Temperature		Time required for frying
	°F	°C	
Cutlets coated with egg and breadcrumbs	360-400	182-204	5-8 minutes
Doughnuts	360-365	182-185	5-8 minutes
Fish cakes	350	177	3-4 minutes
Fritters	375	190	3-5 minutes
Fish, fillets	375	190	4-6 minutes
Fish, whole	375	190	3-5 minutes
Potato chips	375	190	4-8 minutes

Paper: Suitable:

PERSONAL LOANS LIMITED

MONTHLY REPAYMENTS AND TOTALS

Sum Borrowed $	12 months			24 months		
	Interest 23.5%	Amount repaid	Monthly repayment	Interest 23.8%	Amount repaid	Monthly repayment
400	47.96	447.96	37.33	96.08	496.00	20.67
500	60.05	559.80	46.65	120.00	622.08	25.92
700	83.98	783.60	65.30	168.00	866.88	36.12
1000	120.00	1120.32	93.36	240.00	1289.60	51.65
1200	145.00	1342.82	111.90	281.80	1481.80	61.95

Paper: Suitable.   Rule only if requested.

CENTRAL STORES LIMITED
TAKINGS BY DEPARTMENT

Month	DEPARTMENT		
	A	B	C
January	226 000	51 000	45 000
February	127 500	49 750	46 250
March	198 680	50 250	45 320
April	110 250	48 120	44 440
May	170 370	49 200	36 700
June	109 220	48 100	40 200
July	136 200	50 300	46 700
August	120 500	44 700	41 200
September	125 000	41 300	39 700
October	140 200	45 300	40 750
November	180 700	42 400	41 600
December	270 000	55 700	31 200
Total	1 778 420	576 120	449 020

Typist! Please check the totals

Paper: Suitable.

THE BEAUFORT SCALE OF WIND FORCE

Beaufort Number	Wind	Effect	Speed m.p.h.	Speed knots
0	Calm	Wind rises vertically	Less than 1	less than 1
1	Light air	Direction shown by wind only	1-3	1-3
2	Light breeze	Wind felt on face	4-7	4-6
3	Gentle breeze	Leaves in motion	8-12	7-10
4	Moderate breeze	Raises dust	13-18	11-16
5	Fresh breeze	Small trees begin to sway	19-24	17-21
6	Strong breeze	Large branches begin to move	25-31	22-27
7	Moderate gale	Whole trees move	32-38	28-33
8	Fresh gale	Twigs break off trees	39-46	34-40
9	Strong gale	Chimney pots and slates blown off	47-54	41-47
10	Whole gale	Trees uprooted	55-63	48-56
11	Storm	Widespread damage	64-75	57-65
12	Hurrican	Experienced only in the tropics	Over 75	Over 75

Paper: Suitable.

COOKING CHART

Food	Automatic Setting	Shelf position	Time Required (depending on size and weight)
Biscuits	3, 4 or 5	1, 2 or 3	10 - 26 minutes
Bread	7 or 8	3	60 - 75 minutes
Cakes:			
medium rich - 20cm or 22cm	2	3	120 - 150 minutes
plain - 18cm	3	3	75 - 90 minutes
rich fruit - 20cm - 22cm	1	4	240 - 270 minutes
Meringues	1	Base plate	120 minutes
Casserole cooking	3	3	90 - 240 minutes

Allow 10 - 20 minutes pre-heating before placing food in oven

Paper: Suitable. Arrange the MEAT and FISH into alphabetical order.

GRILLING CHART

Food	Switch Position	Grill Position	Time and Notes
MEAT			
Steak (rare) 25mm thick	S	High	3 minutes each side
Steak (average) 25mm thick	F	Low	5-6 minutes each side
Steak (well done)	N	Low	9 minutes each side
Lamb chops	N	Low	5-8 minutes each side
Pork chops	N	Low	7-10 minutes each side
Ham (thick)	N	Low	5-6 minutes each side
Ham (thin)	N	Low	4-6 minutes each side
Bacon	N	Low	Depends on taste
FISH			
Steak and fillets 50mm thick	N	Low	7-10 minutes each side
25mm thick	F	Low	10 minutes
Plaice and Sole	F	Low	10 minutes
Mackerel	N	Low	6 minutes each side
Herring	N	High	10 minutes each side
Kippers	F	Low	3 minutes
TOAST			
Soft in centre	S	High	Grill to degree of colour preferred
Average	F	High	
Crisp	N	High	

Paper: Suitable.

CONVERSION TABLES

millilitres to fluid ounces		fluid ounces to millilitres	
millilitres	fluid oz	fluid oz	millilitres
50	1.75	1	28.41
100	3.51	2	56.82
150	4.26	3	85.24
200	4.03	4	113.65
250	8.48	5	142.66
300	10.54	6	170.47
400	14.04	7	198.89
500	17.58	8	227.30
600	21.10	9	255.41
700	24.63	10	284.24
800	28.14	20	568.24
1000	35.19	40	1136.49

litres to pints and gallons			pints and gallons to litres		
litres	pints	gallons	pints	gallons	litres
$\frac{1}{4}$	0.43	0.05	2	$\frac{1}{4}$	1.13
$\frac{1}{2}$	0.87	0.10	4	$\frac{1}{2}$	2.26
1	1.75	0.21	8	1	4.54
2	3.51	0.42		2	9.09
3	5.42	0.65		3	13.63
4	7.03	0.84		4	18.18
5	8.79	1.10		5	22.73
6	10.55	1.31		6	27.27
7	12.31	1.53		7	31.82
8	14.07	1.75		8	36.36
9	15.83	1.97		9	40.91
10	17.59	2.19		10	45.46